Dear Future Bride

Letters Written By
Nicole McLauchlin

Contributing Letters From
Elder Vanessa Briggs
Rev. Felica Thompson
Pastor Na-Jean Parker

ISBN: 978-1974370979

Preparing Yourself

Dear Future Bride,

As you embark on this new journey of becoming a married woman, you must realize that in order to have a great marriage you must put the Lord first. He must be involved in every aspect of your marriage. Allow the Lord to make you and your husband one in Him. You both need to personally have an intimate relationship with the Lord, so that when the trials of life come, you both will be able to stand and not waiver in your faith in God and in one another. Allow the Holy Spirit to mesh you together as one and always yield to him and he will make your marriage show forth the glory of God, and you will have a godly marriage.

Sincerely,

A Bride Whose Marriage is Yielded to The Lord

~ Mark 10:9
Guest Author: Elder Vanessa Briggs

Dear Future Bride,

Save! Save! Save!

It takes money to not only plan for your wedding, but also for the future of your family. Don't sit around waiting for your knight in shining armor to sweep you off your feet and erase every care in this world.

Don't get me wrong, the man is the provider! It is his job to provide for you, but do not forget that YOU are his partner! YOU are helping to build your house into a healthy home along with him. YOU play a MAJOR role! Don't just sit back and relax! Start a savings account and an emergency fund. Prepare for the future of your family.

Sincerely,

A Bride That Prepares

~ Proverbs 31:13-19

Dear Future Bride,

You may think you will find happiness once you marry the man of your dreams, but are you happy with yourself?

Before you can help, love, and nurture any man or family, you must first know how to love and take care of you! Your well-being and fulfillment does not come from the love of a man, but from the love of God.

Let God take first place, and allow him to be the lover of your soul. He will fill every void, hurt, and pain. When you let him love you, you will be able to love yourself. He will show you how to love your mate and how you both should love each other.

Sincerely,

A Bride Who Loves Herself

~ Matthew 22:37

Dear Future Bride,

If he's willing to "shack" with you and not marry you… MOVE ON!

You don't have time to play house. True love waits and your husband must respect your body because it is the Lord's temple. Your purity is the best wedding gift you can give to your husband. What a great example you will be to your future children, especially your daughters, to let them know that their father was the only one who you laid with.

If you are not a virgin, make it your duty to stay celibate and wait to have sex once you say, "I do." It is what's pleasing to God.

Sincerely,

A Bride Who Waited

~ 1 Corinthians 7:2

Dear Future Bride,

Love is never questionable or unsettled. Make sure you are ready and that you love the man you are going to marry. There is a big difference between cold feet and fear. As you walk down the aisle, be sure it is what you want to do. It's a bad feeling to wonder if you should turn around and make a run for it. Discernment is very important, which means to make clear decisions while being led by the Holy Spirit. If it's meant for you to be married, you will not have a weird feeling in your spirit. You will know it is the right choice, and you will be ready to meet your groom at the altar.

Sincerely,

A Bride Who Was Ready

~ Psalm 119:66

Dear Future Bride,

For those who desire marriage, it is very normal to think about when THE ONE will come. For some the waiting can get tiresome and it's easy to start dating anyone who comes along. I understand you do not want to be by yourself! Companionship is a beautiful thing when it is with the right one. Some females find it hard to wait because they long to be with someone right now and they become impatient. Please do not allow your loneliness to cause you to be connected to the wrong person. I've seen many times women marry the wrong man because they refuse to wait. What's the rush? Wait for the one who will make you smile instead of settling for the one who will make you cry. Your joy and peace of mind is important, and it does not need to be jeopardized just because you can't wait.

Take your time and allow God to prepare the right one for you. Marriage is a big step and the most important words you will say in your life is "I do." So, please take your time!

Sincerely,

A Bride with Patience
~ Romans 8:25

Dear Future Bride,

A lot of women date so they won't feel "alone" or because they are bored. Dating is something that should be taken seriously, and truth be told, you don't need to be involved with just anyone. The purpose of dating is to see who would be considered a potential mate. If you are dating because you are lonely, bored, or want attention, those are the wrong reasons. Some of these dudes are not worth your time. We forget to put our dating lives in God's hands.

I really believe some of our heartbreaks can be prevented if we listen to the voice of God. I often use the word "discernment" because it is so important. Every guy does not have your best interest at heart, and many times they will lure you to believe every word they say, and it is a lie.

God has someone special for you. A man designed to protect, love, and cover you. Keep your guard up, and don't let it down until God leads you to.

Sincerely,

A Bride Who Was Careful

~ 2 Corinthians 6:14

Dear Future Bride,

They say you never know a person until you live with them, and that is the truth!

While you are dating, ask a lot of questions. If you are thinking about getting married, you need to question him as if he was in an interrogation room. Don't be embarrassed or ashamed. After all, this is your life we are talking about!

Your paths may be different, but they should complement each other as you journey this walk of life together. Get background information about his family, job, health benefits, his health, how he spends money, etc.

Get to know his family and see what they are like. You need to know what kind of family you are marrying into.

These components are important, so it is okay to BE NOSEY!

If he is serious about you, he will be honest.

If you feel he's hiding something… RUN!

Sincerely,

A Bride Who Asked a Lot of Questions
~ 1 Thessalonians 5:21 (MSG)

Dear Future Bride,

What's the number one requirement on your list of what you want in a husband? Well, if we think about it physically, the answer for many women could be tall, dark, and handsome. There is nothing wrong with wanting those things. It's great to have someone good to look at every morning when you wake up LOL… but, should that be at the top of your list?

My sister always wanted someone who was tall because she is tall! She used to always say, "I don't want to tower over a short man!" That was what she desired, but God gave her the complete opposite. Her husband is short but loves and treats her like a queen. She did everything she could to turn him down when he kept asking her out on a date. She ignored him and wouldn't answer his calls. She even tried to hook him up with one of our cousins.

LOLOLOL!

But, he never stopped fighting for her. She was so busy looking at his height; she didn't take the time to look at his heart. She finally listened to God and now they have been married for over 10 years and have three beautiful children. When my sister was going through cancer, I saw him take great care of her. Wow, what a real man! Can you imagine what she would have missed out on just because she was worried about his height? She would have missed out on one the greatest blessings of her life. Ladies, the guy you are dating needs to have more going for him than being talk, dark, and handsome.

Sincerely,

A Bride Who Looked Beyond the Physical
~ 1 Peter 3:3-4

Dear Future Bride,

While you are waiting, make sure you are working!

Stop sitting by the telephone hoping the guy in the mall who you gave your number to will give you a call.

Stay busy and get a life.

Go to school, start a career, find something that interests you. There is nothing more unattractive to men than a lazy woman. Do not depend on anyone to take care of every little need and want you have.

You can pay for your own nails, hair, and go shopping with your own money. While you are sitting around wondering when your time will come to get married, you are wasting time. Enjoy your single life.

Take the time to work on being you. When you do get married, you will already know who you are and you won't seek to find your identity in a man.

So, get up and get to work.

Sincerely,

A Working Bride
~ Proverbs 12:11

Dear Future Bride,

Who in the heck put a "time table" on when a woman should get married?

So many women want to get married at a certain age or think they need to hurry up before they get old.

I've said this so many times, but I will say it again! Take your time! There isn't a certain age to say, "I Do!" You may see everyone around you getting married, but you are not them. Wait as long as you need to. If that man isn't sent by God, STAY SINGLE! You can be married at 23 or 53. The only thing that matters is for you to marry the right one.

We serve the one who created time and he will join you to the right man… and it will be perfect timing.

Sincerely,

A Bride on God's Time

~ Ecclesiastes 3:1

Dear Future Bride,

There are a few sayings I'm sure you've heard.

One is "looks can be deceiving" and the other is "never judge a book by its cover." Those sayings are very cliché but are true. Do not be fooled by a smile and good looks. Physical features don't put food on the table, gas in your car, or love you throughout every situation. You can be good looking on the outside, but jacked up on the inside. The heart of the man is what matters. Wolves can dress up in sheep's clothing. He may be fine, but that doesn't mean he is the one.

Sincerely,

A Bride Who Looked Within
~ 1 Samuel 16:7

Dear Future Bride,

The way you dress will give off signals of how you will be treated. If you dress classy, you'll be treated with respect. If you dress showing the body parts men LOVE to see, then you will be treated accordingly. Overexposing yourself is asking for someone to lust after you. You want to attract a man with your brain, not your body. I don't care how saved he is, if all he sees is boobs, butts, and thighs he's not thinking about Jesus. Men are very visual so save the goodies for your hubby!

Sincerely,

A Bride Who Looks Good but Keeps It Covered

~ Romans 12:1-2

Dear Future Bride,

You never know when "Mr. Right" will arrive, so look nice at all times. I know we have our days where we don't feel like dressing up, especially if we just want to go to the store for a second. Please girl, do NOT go to the store or get gas with your hair full of rollers or flexi rods. Don't be seen in pjs, baggy pants, and a big t-shirt. That is not a good look. You may find your husband on aisle three by the meat section so be prepared to show him your best self.

Sincerely,

A Bride Who Dresses to Impress

~ Song of Solomon 4:1

Dear Future Bride,

If you have to explain to your boyfriend why it is important to wait until marriage to have sex, then he is not the one for you. In the dating process, the guy must be aware of your beliefs and morals. Sex before marriage is not pleasing to God. Sex is for a man and woman who made vows of commitment, trust, and love for each other with the exchanging of rings before God and a group of witnesses. Sex with anyone who is not your husband will create "soul ties." In the bible, it does not say that exact word, but it is referred to as when two become one flesh, which can only happen when you have sex. Soul ties can be deadly, dangerous, and difficult to break. But it is beautiful between a husband and wife whom God joins together. Sex connects, binds, and brings oneness to a married couple.

Sex shouldn't be a "hit it and quit it" deal or a "give it to me now so I can feel good" moment. It is a special bond shared with the one you will spend the rest of your life with. So, if your boyfriend doesn't understand the seriousness of sex and why both of you should wait until you are married, walk away because the one God has for you will have those same beliefs and morals. If you have already had sex, starting now ask God for forgiveness and be celibate until your wedding night.

Sincerely,

A Bride Who Waited Until Marriage

~ Mark 10:6-9

Dear Future Bride,

I spoke to you about sex being only for husbands and wives. It is very important to control your emotions and urges for sex. When you are dating, strong feelings are involved. It is easy to have sexual feelings for the person you love. That is why you must be careful.

Group dates help because you are surrounded by other couples and you are not tempted. If you are going out by yourselves, do not stay out too late. The biggest trap is going over to his house or having him come to your house at night. It doesn't matter how saved you are. Your flesh could care less when it wants to be pleased. Many times, women make these mistakes and it causes them to have sex and then feel bad because they knew it was wrong. Keep yourself covered. End your date at a certain time.

Watch out for those heavy make out sessions, which can be accompanied by touching, rubbing, caressing. All it takes is for him to rub you the right way, in the right area, and you are gone. Don't feel bad when you have those feelings. God gave you these feelings to make your sex life with your husband pleasurable. But, do help you and your boyfriend stay on the right track and set boundaries. Be mindful of how late you stay out, how much you touch each other, and be accountable to someone who will keep you in check to make sure you are still living holy. Sex is fun and you will have plenty of it when you are married. Men want sex and lots of it... LOL! So, save it for your husband.

Sincerely,

A Bride Who Avoided Temptation

~ 1 Thessalonians 4:3-5

Dear Future Bride,

The easiest thing to do when dating is to explore ways you can be physically romantic without having sex. Do not put yourself in that position. You may not be having sex, but all the heavy rubbing, groping, and kissing is dangerous territory.

Now, let's talk about oral sex. Yikes! Pretty heavy stuff, huh? This is rarely talked about it. This is probably an embarrassing topic to discuss with an adult, if you are a teenager reading this letter. A lot of times some people use oral sex as an excuse to unleash their sexual desires so they can have pleasure. This way they can still be pleased and not disobey God's principles when it comes to sex and marriage.

Stay away from all sexual immortality!

If you have to think about whether it is right or wrong, then it's wrong.

Stop exploring the different ways you can please your body and refrain from sexual sin. Be patient. Once you say, "I do," then you can have sex!

Sincerely,

A Bride Who Knows the Feeling of Being Curious

~ Hebrews 13:4

Preparing For The Wedding

Dear Future Bride,

Congratulations on your engagement!

I know that you are excited, anticipating marrying the love of your life and planning the wedding of your dreams. I know that you are looking forward to your happily ever after, but before you enter this most sacred covenant, I'd like to ask you a question. "Are you ready to step into the helpmate chapter of your life?"

There are three very important roles of a successful helpmate that I'd like to share with you. A successful helpmate prays for her husband, makes him a priority in her life and pushes him to levels that he never imagined he could go. Being a helpmate to your husband is an important assignment and calling from God. I know you're thinking that anyone can help someone else, but the help that you will give your husband can literally change his life, and make his life so much easier.

The first role of your assignment is to pray for your husband. Pray that he fears God and will seek God and be led by God as he leads you and your family. Pray that God will keep his mind stayed on Him, his body healed and his spirit obedient to His voice. Pray that God will give you the wisdom to know when it's time to give some alone time to listen to the voice of God and plan to carry out God's plan for your household.

Pray that God connects him with other men of God that can mentor him, and those whom he himself can mentor.

The second role of your assignment as a helpmate is to make him your priority. Now, I know that there are many wives and soon to be wives that don't agree with this role, but I'm telling you what makes a happy husband. Listen to me close, when your husband knows that after your relationship with God, pleasing him is your priority, that man will feel like he can do ANYTHING!

You see in so many areas of his, he has been compared to others; on the job, in his circle of friends and even in his family. Yet in his relationship with you, he is not only your man, he is "THE MAN," and there is no greater motivation.

The third role of your assignment as a helpmate is to be prepared to push your husband. Please don't be fooled to think that men don't have depressing days, because they do. You may be the only person in his life that knows when he is going through this, so it is your responsibility as his helpmate to push him during these times. Your encouragement is so important to how he sees himself as a man. Hundreds of people can encourage him, but if he doesn't receive that affirmation from you, all those other words will fall on deaf ears. When you share with him how much you believe in him that pushes him to be even better.

So, as you plan the ceremony of a lifetime, don't forget to ponder the three important yet simple roles of this next chapter of your life. Pray for your husband daily, always make him a priority, and push him past his comfort zone, so that he can reach the destiny that God has planned for him.

Sincerely,

A bride who prays for her husband, makes him her priority and pushes him to pursue his dreams

~ Genesis 2:18

Guest Author: Rev. Felica Raines Thompson, First Lady

Dear Future Bride,

If you plan on having a reception, do not feel bad if you cannot invite everyone!

The reception is the most expensive part of a wedding budget. Only invite those whom you really want to be a part of your celebration. I don't care how much money other women are spending. Don't you dare go broke over a wedding!

Life happens after everything is over. If there are people who get mad because they are not invited, brush it off. At the end of the day, you and your husband-to-be are paying for their plate, NOT them.

Trust me, they'll get over it. Besides, most of them won't buy you a gift anyway!

Sincerely,

A Bride on a Budget

~ Proverbs 21:5

Dear Future Bride,

Don't be so caught up in the fantasy world of love that you ignore "red flags" in your relationship. If you have a prayer life and are sensitive to the Holy Spirit, those red flags are warnings from him.

LISTEN!

USE YOUR DISCERNMENT!

Your prayer concerning your relationship should be for God to reveal those things that can be an issue in your marriage. Pray and ask God to show you the heart of your future husband. If he shows you a warning, don't ignore that feeling.

Listen!

Sincerely,

A Watchful Bride

~ Hebrews 3: 7-8

Dear Future Bride,

Your wedding day will be one of the most memorable moments of your life. Make it special. If you are like me, you are going to want to do everything yourself. There is a saying, "If you want something right, do it yourself," and that is fine. But, it is okay to ask for help. After you get engaged, some of these questions are sure to pop in your head: Do I want a big wedding or a small wedding? Do I want a long list of guests or a private intimate wedding with just family and friends? What are my colors? How many will be in my bridal party? How much money do I want to spend on food?

Calm down!

Relax!

Breathe!

I know how you are feeling. This is why I said you need help.

Before you look for a wedding planner, write out what you want and how much you would like to spend.

After you have written down some thoughts, let your wedding planner do the work! That's what you are paying them for, right?

Sincerely,

A Bride Who Had Awesome Wedding Planners

~ Proverbs 15:22

Dear Future Bride,

When you choose your bridal party, be VERY selective!

Those who take part in your special day should be the ones who support, encourage, and love you. They are the ones who should stay prayerful for your union. Always have those in your corner who are there to celebrate your marriage. Like the old saying goes, "Birds of a feather, flock together!"

Sincerely,

A Watchful Bride

~ Proverbs 18:24

Dear Future Bride,

You are not married yet!

It is not your job to take on the responsibilities of a wife! Right now, you are duty free.

Don't get me wrong, it is fine to support your fiancé. If he needs your help, do what you can. But please remember, there are some jobs that you only do as his wife. Stop doing his laundry, taking care of his bills, or any other things that you are not meant to handle right now. You are the fiancé.

After you say, "I do," that's when you can go ahead and get to work.

Sincerely,

A Bride with A Ring on It

~ Galatians 6:5

Dear Future Bride,

Have fun when planning your wedding!

It doesn't have to be stressful. Yes, it can be very tiresome and tedious, but there are some joys while planning for your big day.

My favorite part of planning was the cake testing. It was fun meeting with our cake lady and trying out different flavors, icing, and even picking out the design.

Make it even more fun by getting your fiancé involved. Bring him along while running errands and you will be amazed at how close you guys will become during this process. So, don't stress, make it fun for the both of you.

Sincerely,

A Bride Who Has Fun

~ Ecclesiastes 8:15

Dear Future Bride,

Before you say, "I do," marriage counseling is a must!

It doesn't matter how much you think you know about marriage, it is best to sit down and talk to someone with experience. You can't take marriage advice from everyone. Know who to talk and listen to. Marriage is one of the biggest steps you will take in your life, so it is important to know what lies ahead of you and your mate. A good counselor will tell you the good, the bad, and the ugly parts of marriage. Marriage counseling will also show you how serious the decision you are making is and help you to figure out if you are prepared to go into this phase of your life.

You will find out a lot about your fiancé, but you will also find out a lot about yourself.

Truth be told, you are not as perfect as you think you are.

Be willing to listen and take constructive criticism from someone who is trying to help your marriage be a success. Everyone needs great advice!

Sincerely,

A Bride Who Listened

~ Proverbs 19:20

Dear Future Bride,

The big question while planning a wedding is what kind of wedding do you want? Do you want a big one or a small one? Do you want a huge bridal party or just you and your husband at the altar? Again, it's all about what your vision is and how much you want to spend. You don't have to spend a lot of money to have a beautiful wedding. Find deals, friends, and hook ups. I was blessed to have a cost-efficient wedding, continue to pay my bills, and eat! It's not about how much money you spend, it's about whom you are spending the rest of your life with. Remember, your ceremony only lasts for a couple of hours. Your marriage is for a lifetime. Are you ready to make that big step?

Sincerely,

A Bride Who Found Good Deals

~ Proverbs 21:5

Preparing For Marriage

Dear Future Bride,

So, you're preparing for the "big day" there must be so much going through your mind!

Everyone wants to plan the "perfect wedding" and it can be so exhausting and trying. Almost every bride feels this pressure because it's one of the most important experiences of your life.

But dear lady don't let the details overwhelm you! Most brides believe that if this day is not completely perfect it's an indication that the marriage won't be either. Well I've got news for you, just as it takes work to make your wedding day a success it will take work to make the marriage a success. So, plan for the best and work through the hitches! Don't let stress and worry about what can go wrong cloud your day. Just breathe and pray. If everything isn't perfect, it's ok!

Oftentimes times it's our thoughts that overshadow the experience. If you allow them to, your thoughts can really consume you. Our thoughts become so focused on the tasks what we must do to accomplish that day, we find it difficult and almost impossible to think about anything else.

However, leading up to the day and even as you go through the day, catch your thoughts and anxieties that are contrary to God's will. Don't allow them to control your mind and your heart. Replace your negative thoughts with this scripture: "For the weapons of our warfare are not carnal but mighty in God for pulling down strongholds, casting down arguments and every high thing that exalts itself against the knowledge of God, bringing every thought into captivity to the obedience of Christ." (2 Corinthians 10:4-5)

Every marriage is unique and every wedding day will be as well. It's up to you God and your husband to create a wonderful life and relationship not just a wonderful day. So, in your planning remember to include these things:

1. Discuss not only the details of the wedding day but discuss the details of what you will two want to see happen in everyday relationship. Talk about fears, doubts, likes, dislikes, differences and commonalities. Discuss and compare the Vision you both have the union. The bible says, "Can two walk together, except they be agreed?" Amos 3:3

2. Take time for pre-marital counseling. This is a detail that many couples leave out but it will help you to save your marriage before it begins. A good counselor will help you discuss intricacies that we tend to overlook such as how we will handle finances, family (immediate and extended, please note in laws play a great role in our marriages) and future personal goals and plans. Counseling will allow you to communicate through important details to make sure "you do" understand the covenant of your marriage before you say, "I do." Marriage is two individuals from two different experiences uniting as one. Therefore, it doesn't matter how much preparation you make for the big day if you don't prepare for every day, the marriage will not last! For the bible tells us "The wise are mightier than the strong, and those with knowledge grow stronger and stronger.

So, don't go to war without wise guidance; victory depends on having many advisers. Prov 24:5-6. 3.

Last but most importantly, include God in every detail. Ecclesiastes 4:12: "Though one may be overpowered, two can defend themselves. A cord of three strands is not quickly broken."

Before you have visited all the wedding planning websites and watched all the wedding planning, prior to having read all the perfect wedding magazines and constructing images and ideas about what you must do to make the perfect wedding day; visit the bible and pray. God has the greatest picture ever of what this day and every day of the rest of your married life should be.

Dear future bride, take from a bride who has been married for over 23 years that although this day is important it's not as important as all the other days of your marriage that will follow.

Therefore, focus more on the days after the wedding day than the wedding day itself.

Sincerely,

A bride who chose to forgo perfect traditional wedding and happily had a perfect justice of the peace wedding

~ Proverbs 24:5-6

Guest Author: Pastor Na-Jean Parker

Dear Future Bride,

It is very easy to look at other couples and admire them. Often, I find it is easy to start looking at my own marriage and begin to wonder "why can't my husband be like my friend's husband?"

There is nothing wrong with looking to couples as role models, but do not compare your marriage with anyone else's. Every marriage is different and unique. What looks good in public may not be the case in private.

You will never know the private struggles and issues that other couples face. So don't put their marriages on a pedestal.

Be grateful for the man God has given you. He may not be perfect, but neither are you.

The grass is never greener on the other side; in fact it may not be real!

Sincerely,

A Bride Who's Thankful for The Man She Has

~ Philippians 4: 12-13

Dear Future Bride,

Marriage takes work!

Once you get married, it's not just about you anymore. A lot of people think marriage is all about sex... sex... sex... and more sex! Marriage is more than sex.

I will admit that sex is icing on the cake, but you should have a cake already baked before you can think about putting the icing on.

Marriage is about commitment, responsibility, compromise, and dedication. Those elements take a lot of work. If you aren't willing to put in the work, you may not be ready to bake a cake.

Sincerely,

A Bride Who Bakes

~ Proverbs 16:3

Dear Future Bride,

Prayer is one of the keys to a successful marriage.

Get on your knees and pray for your marriage, children, and everything that involves the well being of your husband and household. Stop complaining and start praying. When God is the center, everything will fall in line!

Before you pray about the issues concerning your marriage, pray for yourself. Ask God to make you the best wife and mother for your husband and family. During your time of dating, it is crucial that you pray. A woman that prays will save her entire house.

Sincerely,

A Bride That Prays
~ Mark 11:24

Dear Future Bride,

Men need encouragement. It is important to build up and celebrate your man. There is nothing worse than a nagging, negative wife.

As his wife, it is your job to speak life over your husband even if you feel that he's not doing what he needs to do. If he hears from your mouth that you love him and you stand behind him, eventually your words will line up with his actions. Tell him he is the best thing that's ever happened to you. He needs to hear those things.

In marriage, you may face difficult times, but keep speaking the word to him and over him. Let him know he's going to make it and everything is going to be alright.

When he sees you stand by him, it will make him push for you and your family.

Sincerely,

A Bride Who Encourages Her Husband

~ Proverbs 31:11-12

Dear Future Bride,

You are your husband's number one cheerleader!

Support him in every endeavor he puts his hands to. Even if you think it's not important or it is something that is not of interest to you, be behind him and show you care. My husband is a pastor and every single time he preaches I'm his biggest cheerleader in his "amen corner." He can always count on me to be in the audience smiling at him or yelling, "PREACH IT!"

It does something for a man when they know you are rooting for them. My husband knows he can always count on me to be there for him and to have his back.

Men may seem hard on the exterior, but on the inside, they need love, affirmation, and honor because that is what keeps them going and working hard for you.

Remember, if you don't support your husband, someone else will… and you better not let that happen on your watch!

Sincerely,

A Bride Who Supports Her Man
~ Ephesians 5:22-23

Dear Future Bride,

My husband is my best friend!

We share everything. When you are married to the one God has for you, marriage is beautiful. Will he get on your nerves? YES! LOL!

When you are dating you can go to your own separate houses and have space until the next time you see each other, but when you are married it's you and him forever. There is no such thing as "I need my space." You might want to rethink getting married if you still feel you are required to have your own space, because that ain't happening when you are under the same roof LOL. But, if you are with the right one, you won't mind at all.

We laugh together, go to the movies together, and my favorite… Netflix and midnight slushy runs to Sonic! You don't only share good times together, but bad times, and mournful times.

When my father was on his deathbed, my husband was right by my side holding me through the night when I was grieving and cried myself to sleep.

That's what marriage is all about. Through the ups and downs, you can always count on each other in this thing we call "life." So, enjoy the ride. It's amazing!

Sincerely,

A Happy Bride
~ Genesis 2:18

Dear Future Bride,

If you really want knowledge about "real life" marriage, surround yourself with women who have been married for a long time. They have stood the test of time. Ask questions and find out some of the things that helped make it last. Of course, times have changed and we are in a new era but if someone can stay married to the same man for over ten years, they are doing something right. If my father was still alive, my parents would be celebrating their 50th wedding anniversary. I think about how long that is and I am in awe! Marriage is for the mature. It is not for the selfish. Get advice from older couples! I'm sure they have some amazing tips that can help you.

Sincerely,

A Bride Still Seeking Advice

~ Titus 2:4-5

Dear Future Bride,

Let me warn you! The first thing people are going to ask you after you get married is, "are you ready for the babies?" It is so annoying! I still get asked this question. And don't let them say, "What's taking you so long?"

Well, put your mind at ease and take your time. Don't allow people to rush you. Just like saying "I do" is a big step, so is starting a family. Kids are expensive. They are a blessing, but they are an expensive blessing… LOL. I wonder if people stop and realize the increase in their budget once children are involved. Formula, diapers, wipes, baby powder, clothes, daycare, food… oh, my goodness! It's a lot to take on if you are not prepared. When you are ready to have kids, it is okay. If you are not ready to have kids, that is okay too.

Besides, the ones rushing you to have kids will be the ones missing when it's time to buy formula or rock your crying youngin' to sleep at 3:00 am.

Sincerely,

A Bride Who Loves Children but Does Not Mind Taking Her Time

~ Psalm 113:9

Dear Future Bride,

There will be moments in your marriage when you will have to learn how to accept the decisions made by your husband. Some decisions you may not understand or agree with, but you should let him take the lead of your household. Now, I'm not saying don't voice your opinion. As his wife, a lot of times you may have a different perspective. They need to hear what you have to say because that is what we do as wives. Your job is to pray for your husband and ask God to lead him to make the right decisions. There are some cases where God will show you how to say certain things if you disagree with him. God will open his heart and he will accept the advice you give. Remember, if you disagree with a decision he's making, go to God in prayer and if it's wrong, God will handle it.

But, if the decision is right, you should trust the decision he makes through the help of God.

Sincerely,

A Bride Who Learned How to Trust

~ Proverbs 3:5-6

Dear Future Bride,

One of the biggest lies that you can tell yourself is, "If I marry him, maybe he will change."

Yes, women have influence and we are known to bring about change, but there are some things only God can change about that man. There may be certain habits, tendencies, and awkward ways that have been a part of him before you came along.

If he always left the cap off the toothpaste, then he is going to continue to do it now. If he's always been messy, then don't be surprised if he is still messy. If he's always had a bad temper and it was not dealt with as a child then it will follow him into adulthood.

You must take off the "Wonder Woman" outfit and realize there are some things you are not going to change.

Childhood hurts, self-esteem issues, and certain pains from his past can be in his present, and God can fix those things.

We do have an advantage though! Anything we desire for our husband can be petitioned through prayer as we get on our knees and call on the name of Jesus for our husband. God can fix anything, and there is nothing too hard for him. Continue to pray with your whole heart and watch God move. If you want something about your husband to change, let God handle it!

Sincerely,

A Bride Who Serves a God Who Can Do Anything

~ Jeremiah 32:27

Dear Future Bride,

Marriage will require both of you to work.

One of the decisions you will have to come in agreement with is how the house will run. All responsibilities should not be on you or him.

For example, you may not like cleaning, but your husband might. You may love cooking, so that may be your part you take on. I knew before I married my husband that cleaning was not his "thing", but he LOVES to cook. As a matter of fact, he cooks better than me. In our house, he does the cooking and I do the cleaning. That way we are both happy and get what we want.

Now, sometimes you may have to compromise and help with each other's duties if things get hectic with your schedules, and that's ok.

Help each other and then get back on your assigned duties.

Sincerely,
A Bride Who Worked as a Team with Her Husband

~ Galatians 6:2

Dear Future Bride,

The words "I love you" are powerful words!
Some couples will say it in relationship after
relationship because they assume it is what
everyone is supposed to say when you are
dating. Love is more than a feeling and it's more
than a sexual desire. Don't get me wrong,
feelings are a big part of love, but it is not the
main component. Love is a decision. If your
husband makes you mad, you love him no
matter what little stupid thing he's done. Love
is taking care of your spouse when he gets sick,
loses his job, and even when he has hurt you.
You must choose to love. My mother took care
of my father when he was diagnosed with
cancer. Every day she had to feed, bathe, and
clothe him. Did she feel like giving up at times
because it was too much? I'm pretty sure she
did. There were probably times she wanted to
cry herself to sleep because the work load of

caring for my sick daddy was a lot. What kept her going? It was her love for him. If I may paraphrase, one specific line in the wedding vows state will you care for her or him until death do us part. That's exactly what my mom did. She cared for my daddy and she never left his side. My sisters and I were with my mother at my daddy's hospital bed as we watched him take his last breath. Love is not selfish, but it is selfless. Please remember that before you say, "I do."

Sincerely,

A Bride Who Really Loves Her Husband

~ 1 Corinthians 13:4-7

Dear Future Bride,

Date night is so important!

Life can be hectic with jobs, school, ministry, and even when you start having children. Don't be so busy that you don't find time for yourselves.

For my husband and me, our day is Monday. Because my husband is a pastor, he is on the job throughout the week at all hours of the day. So, we decided that every Monday is just for us. Since we love watching movies and TV together, we call it "Movie Monday."

Movies during the matinee hour are a good price for couples that are trying to save money (hint, hint). So, after our movie, we go out to dinner to one of our favorite spots.

Do something you like to do on date night. If you guys plan it, you will have something to look forward to in your week. Date night will help you keep the spark in your marriage and will also continue to bring you closer together.

At the end of the day, you guys have each other forever, so have fun!

Sincerely,

A Bride Who Enjoys Quality Time with Her Man

~ Ecclesiastes 9:9

Dear Future Bride,

Because you will spend a lifetime with your husband, take the time to learn everything that makes him who he is.

What is his favorite color, food, or sports team?

Do you know what size shoe he wears?

What are his fears?

Is he scared of heights?

What is he allergic to?

If you can remember one thing that annoys him, could you?

These are questions you will have time to learn while dating. Don't feel like you have to know it all by a certain time. You have the rest of your lives for him to know you and for you to know him. Be observant and learn everything you can. This will help with knowing what surprise gifts to give him, or even knowing what not to say concerning a certain area that might be sensitive to talk about.

Watch him and learn all you can!

Sincerely,

A Bride Who is Still Learning About Her Husband

~ Proverbs 18:15

Dear Future Bride,

Men are clueless when it comes to knowing what makes us feel certain ways. It's not their fault.

It's the way God made them... LOL.

It is our job to communicate with them effectively. They are not mind readers and we can't assume they will automatically know what goes on in our brain. You must be able to share your feelings. If he hurt you, tell him so he will know! If he made you feel special and appreciated, let him know so that he can see how much you appreciate him!

You have to talk to him so he can know what is going on in your mind and your emotions. It will help him become a better husband to you.

Sincerely,

A Bride Who Is Still Working on Her Communication

~ Proverbs 12:25

Dear Future Bride,

Whatever you do, do not disrespect your husband. Treat him like the king he is. There is nothing more disgusting than a woman who talks badly about her husband, not only in his face, but also behind his back. If he's tripping or he's not acting accordingly to the word of God, continue to speak highly about him. With your prayers and the positive declarations that you speak over his life, he will be what God has called him to be. If he's not there yet, keep treating him as though he is. Tell him he looks good. Tell him that he's the best thing that has ever happened to you. That does wonders for a man's self-esteem.

One of the things I will always appreciate about a good friend of mine is the way she spoke about her ex-husband to her children. Now ladies, if I were to go by emotions, my friend had every right to talk about her ex-husband because of all of the things he put her through.

He treated her terribly and put her through so much pain and misery. Despite what she went through, she never spoke about how she felt to her kids. They never heard a bad word about their daddy out of her mouth. If my friend was willing to do that for her ex-husband, you should be able to respect your husband in his rightful position as the head of the house. When he sees the respect you give him, don't worry… he'll do a complete turn around.

Sincerely,

A Bride Who Speaks Highly of Her Husband

~ Ephesians 5:22-24

Dear Future Bride,

Never argue in public!

It is very embarrassing to get into a fight in a public setting. Save that for the house. There are people who want your marriage to fail because of jealousy and they get joy from chaos. Don't give them anything to talk about. What goes on in your house, stays in your house.

Also, never argue in front of your children. Growing up as a child, I never heard my parents arguing. Children are very observant and will pay attention to everything. Show them how marriage is supposed to work. Your marriage will be the example on how they will pattern their marriage.

Be a good example!

Sincerely,

A Bride Who Keeps Her Martial Business to Herself

~ 1 Thessalonians 4:11-12

Dear Future Bride,

Sometimes as women, we talk too much. This can be a turn off for your husband. What I mean by talking too much is in the sense of nagging. Nagging and complaining will not get you anywhere. Your husband will tune you out. There is a time to speak and a time to be quiet. We don't have to go back and forth all the time. We can get our point across without being loud or "ratchet." Your husband will never listen to you with that kind of approach. You don't want to annoy him, you want him to listen!

Sincerely,

A Bride with a Controlled Tongue

~ Proverbs 21:9

Dear Future Bride,

You have to recognize which battles are meant to be fought or lost. You are not going to win every argument.

Be a big girl and realize that sometimes you may be wrong. You are not going to be right all the time. There may be some battles that you could have fought and won, but sometimes it is just better to be quiet.

Is winning an argument just to say, "I told you so" worth not having peace in your household? If you are right about certain things and your husband is still not listening to you, pray!

I'm pretty sure you are noticing that I use prayer a lot. It is because it works. If you are right, God will convict your husband and will cause him to apologize. I have seen it happen for me plenty of times. God will show your husband his mistake. If he is a good man and fears the Lord, your husband will come to you and apologize.

Instead of fighting the battles yourself, give it to the Lord.

Sincerely,

A Bride Who Turns Everything Over to Jesus

~ Exodus 14:14 (NLT)

Dear Future Bride,

Make your home a place of rest, peace, and love. Every man wants to come home to a calm and soothing place after a hard day of work. You can create that for him. You may even want to have his favorite meal ready, a nice hot bath for the two of you, and some cuddle time where he can just lay in your lap and talk about everything the day threw at him. A massage, foot rub, or laying in your lap can be such a comfort to him. Your home should never be a place they want to avoid. When he knows his house is a place of serenity, he will rush home to you.

Sincerely,

A Bride Who Makes Her House a Happy Home

~ Proverbs 14:1

Dear Future Bride,

You are not going to do everything perfectly. It doesn't matter how long you've been married. Wives are learning how to be better every day. There is always something to learn about your husband and yourself. Don't compare how your marriage operates with other women and their marriages. Be who you are and be the wife God has called you to be for your husband. You can't be the kind of wife your best friend is because your best friend's ways will not work for your husband. God will mold you into the wife he has called you to be. He's so faithful, righteous, and just. We serve a perfect God, and he knows what he is doing!

Sincerely,

A Bride Who Still Makes Mistakes

~ Deuteronomy 32:4

Dear Future Bride,

As I write my last letter, it is my hope that these fifty letters were a help to you. While dating, you may find yourself rereading these letters, and that is exactly what I want you to do. I don't claim to know it all, but I do realize what God has called me to do and that is be here for you.

I pray you will take these nuggets and use them to help you. Marriage is beautiful, exciting, fun, difficult, annoying, and even chaotic. But with the Father, Son, and the Holy Spirit in your marriage, you will succeed. In Matthew 6:33, the Bible tells us to "seek ye first the kingdom of God, and his righteousness; and all these things shall be added unto you."

One of those things is your marriage. Lean on God for everything. Pray for your husband before you meet him. Your husband is out there right now, and I'm pretty sure he can't wait to meet you!

Sincerely,

A Bride Who Is Here for Future Brides

~ Mathew 6:33

Nicole McLauchlin

Nicole McLauchlin is a native of Fayetteville, North Carolina. Nicole graduated from Methodist University with a degree in music education and a Master's degree in Music Education with a concentration in Voice.

Nicole is married to Pastor Brandon McLauchlin and together they serve faithfully at St. Charles AME Zion Church in Sparkill, New York. Along with her music ministry, Nicole strongly believes her call is to encourage, build, and uplift young women by showing them how important it is to find their purpose in Jesus Christ.